TAKING THE NEXT STEP

LEADER GUIDE

A GUIDE
FOR
NEW
CHURCH
MEMBERS

JERRI HERRING

ABOUT THE AUTHOR

Jerri Herring is Leadership Development
Consultant in the General Leadership Associational
Leadership Team of the Field Service Section in the
Ministry and Leadership Development Department of
The Baptist Sunday School Board.

Copyright 1996 • Convention Press 5120-33
All Rights Reserved
Reprinted 1997

Dewey Decimal Classification number 254.5
Subject Heading: Church Membership
ISBN # 0-8054-9441-3

Printed in the United States of America
Available from Customer Service Center
1-800-458-2772
and Baptist Book Stores

Ministry Leadership Development Department
Bible Teaching-Reaching Division
The Sunday School Board of the Southern Baptist
Convention
127 Ninth Avenue, North
Nashville, Tennessee 37234-0163

Acknowledgements:
Scripture quotations marked NIV are from the Holy Bible,
New International Version © copyright 1973, 1978, 1984
by International Bible Society

**TABLE
OF
CONTENTS**

INTRODUCTION

To the Leader:

Helping people become assimilated into the life and ministry of a church is a priority for growing churches. Some of the people who need help taking the next step toward meaningful involvement in the church are:
1. Persons interested in becoming Christians or members of your church;
2. New Christians;
3. Transfers from other congregations;
4. Persons who dropped out of active church participation and are now returning.

New Christians have special needs:
- They have limited or no understanding of the Bible
- The abyss separating the unchurched world and the churched world is deep. They have crossed this abyss by faith in Jesus—bringing a lot of the misunderstanding, doubts, fears, behavior, and secular view of that lost world with them.

In order to effectively assimilate new members into your church family, it is important not to assume that people transferring from other congregations have an adequate understanding of their faith and church membership. They may have as much need of the basic things as those who are strangers to our faith and church life. Therefore, *Taking the Next Step: A Guide for New Church Members* and *Taking the Next Step Leader Guide* deal with basic Christian concepts as well as facts about membership in your particular church.

It is hoped that this material will be a valuable tool as your church assimilates new members; strengthens new Christians; and they, in turn, strengthen your church. I pray that this will be a meaningful study for both the new member and for you.

This leader guide is for your use as you prepare to lead each of the five sessions. The material is written so that it may be used by churches of any size. As with all teaching plans, it is not possible to provide everything you need to conduct these sessions. If you will carefully follow the procedures you will see suggestions and reminders of things that you will need to prepare or provide for that particular session.

You may want to consider offering two different classes for new members.

• *A believer's class.*—For persons interested in becoming Christians or members of your church; for new Christians; for transfers from other congregations; for persons who have dropped out of active participation in a church and are now returning to church.

• *A membership (newcomers, seekers, inquirers) class.*—For persons interested in becoming Christians; for persons interested in transferring from another congregation (especially those from congregations or denominations that are different from your church); for persons who do not reveal their spiritual or church relationship, but indicate interest in knowing more about the basics of coming into your church.

Suggestions for Using This Material

• It is recommended that each session last one hour. You will need to determine how much time you wish to place on each item in the session presentation.

• Read all of the student material before you begin

planning for this new member class. The preparation section for each session lists the things that you will need to prepare prior to each session.

• The leader of this class should either be a staff person or a lay member who is familiar with the workings and organization of your church, the functions of the church, and the biblical references.

• For this study to be most effective, the sessions should be studied consecutively. If the study is to be held at church (on Sunday morning, Sunday evening, or Wednesday evenings) check your church calendar to ensure there are five consecutive weeks available before you schedule your study. If the book is to be studied in a home or other location away from church, make certain that the location is available and the dates/times are open.

• Enlist several persons to be prayer partners and encouragers throughout these sessions.

• Relax! Your plans are in place, the participants have been enlisted, and you are ready to begin leading one of the most important classes your church has ever provided. This book will emphasize the fact that God has a plan for every Christian, and He will provide wonderful results!

OTHER IDEAS:

There are several ways this material can be used effectively. You may choose to use more than one of these plans and then decide which works best for your church. (Remember that each session is intended to last one hour.)

• IDEA 1:

This material can be used for five consecutive weeks—meeting one hour each week during Bible study (Sunday School) time. You will need to reserve a room that may be used for each of these five sessions.

• IDEA 2:

This material can be used during a lunchtime setting after a Sunday morning worship and Bible study hour. Consider meeting in the fellowship hall or a similar room in your church. The study may be done for five consecutive weeks or once a month for five months.

• IDEA 3:

This material may be studied for five consecutive weeks in the home of the leader or another church member.

• IDEA 4:

This material may be used in a retreat setting either at the church or off campus. The informality of a retreat is appealing to most people. (Getting away from the church may help some new members feel more comfortable in asking questions.) Take the time to work up an agenda that includes meals, breaks, and a time for fellowship. Provide a map or transportation for each person planning to attend the retreat.

• IDEA 5:

This material may be studied on Sunday evenings. Notify the Sunday School classes where these new members will be assigned so that they can be encouragers for this study. As in the Sunday morning setting, be sure to reserve a room that is available for five consecutive weeks.

WHO AM I?

PREPARATION:

• Provide nametags, copies of *Taking the Next Step: A Guide for New Church Members*, paper, and pencils.

• If this class is being conducted in a home or retreat setting, plan to serve simple refreshments.

• Read carefully all of *Taking the Next Step: A Guide for New Church Members*—to become familiar with each chapter. Read through this leader guide to determine how much time needs to be given to each of the suggested procedures. (Time should be allotted according to the number of participants, the maturity level of the group, and the setting.)

PROCEDURE:

1. As members arrive, give out nametags. Allow time to introduce each participant and ask them to share an interesting fact about themselves. It is important that the members of the group feel comfortable with each other.

• Distribute copies of *Taking the Next Step: A Guide for New Church Members*. Share the reasons for this new members' class and explain how the sessions will progress.

At this time point out your expectations for the group (working through the process, interaction with others in the group, homework, and so on).

2. Overview the purpose statement for chapter 1, "Who Am I?" Point out that Genesis 1:27 reminds us that God created us in His image and He created us to have a relationship with Him. Then explain that our Christian lives may be compared to a sort of time line: We stand at one end of the continuum and (hopefully) progress across the time line toward spiritual maturity.

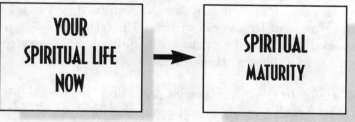

Point out the importance of each person determining where he or she is in their spiritual growth so they may begin to look at where they would like to be in one week, one month, or one year. Explain that this maturation is a process that involves disciplines of daily prayer, Bible study, worship, and discipleship. These lead to the actions of witnessing, fellowshipping, missions, and ministry.

3. Ask conferees to turn to page 6 of the member book. Read aloud the definition of *to repent* and ask each person to circle the response they believe is correct. Ask four volunteers to read aloud these four Scripture passages—2 Corinthians 7:10; Acts 8:12; Colossians 2:13-14; Galatians 2:20. The correct response is: (d.): *Repentance is a change of mind,*

heart, will, and the way you live. Ask those who made a wrong choice to mark the correct response in their books.

4. Say: Faith in Christ makes the difference between being a Christian and merely doing Christian things. Direct members to turn to page 7 of the book and complete the list of good things that are done by persons who are not Christians. Ask a volunteer to read aloud Ephesians 2:8. (*For it is by grace you have been saved, through faith—and this not from yourselves, it is the gift of God—not by works, so that no one can boast.*) Emphasize the importance of this verse in their Christian lives— especially as they begin to seek their place of service as new members in the church.

5. Refer to the "promises of salvation" on pages 8-9, and ask each person to write out the four promises in their own words. *These are found in Romans 8:1-3; John 3:16; Philippians 1:6; and John 10:27-28.* If your group is large, consider forming four teams and assign one Scripture to each team to rewrite and report on. After work is completed, call for sharing.

6. State that each person is an important part of the church family; part of their responsibility is to share with others the salvation experiences they have had. Direct each participant to write out his or her testimony in the space provided in the book. Encourage them to keep the testimonies short and simple. Allow time to complete work, then divide into pairs and ask each person to share the testimony with his or her partner.

7. Point out that each person is part of a network of friends and acquaintances to whom they can witness daily. Encourage each participant to keep a journal as they read the Bible and have daily quiet times. Give out several sheets of paper or a prepared notebook as incentive to maintain the journal. Ask them to write down the names of people from their personal network and the results of their witnessing opportunities. Explain that no one will be looking over their shoulder or asking them to read from these notebooks in class, but keeping this journal is excellent discipline to promote spiritual maturity.

8. Stress to conferees the importance of being actively involved in their church. As a new member, each person has a vital role to fulfill. Help them to understand the need: to become involved in the ministries of the church; to become a part of a group of three or more people whom they consider friends; and to become a disciple who leads others to accept Christ and helps them develop as a maturing Christian. (This is a wonderful opportunity to explain the importance of the small group Bible study experience we call Sunday School.)

9. Ask members to turn to the glossary at the back of the book. Briefly review the terms that apply to this first session and ask if there are any questions or comments about each one. Clarify the definitions, if necessary.

10. Close with a "teaser" about session 2 that will encourage the study of the session. Close with prayer that each person will make a commitment to be a consistent and courageous church member.

ANSWERS FOR CHAPTER 1

Genesis 1:27—*(image)*; Romans 6:23a—*(death)*;
Romans 6:23b—*(life)*; Romans 8:1-3—
(condemnation), *(sin)* *(death)*, *(Son)*, *(sin)*; Biblical
repentance—(d) is the correct answer; Matthew
3:11—*(repentance)*, *(believes)*;
Hebrews 10:14—*(made perfect forever)*;
John 6:37—*(never drive away.)*;
Romans 8:1-3—*(Spirit of life)*, *(law of sin and
death)*; John 3:16—*(believes)*, *(eternal life)*;
Philippians 1:6—*(carry it on to completion)*;
John 10:28—*(snatch them out of my hand)*;
2 Corinthians 3:18—(transformed);
1 Peter 2:21—*(in his steps)*.

WHAT IS THE CHURCH?

PREPARATION:

• Have on hand a copy of your church budget that shows the percentages your church is currently giving to foreign, home, and local missions; a listing of any special support groups that your church sponsors; and copies of the mission statement of your church. (If your church does not have a mission statement, consider using this class to develop one in step 6. The Great Commission is an appropriate focus for the mission statement—the vision statement will be the way your church plans to carry out the Great Commission.)

• If this class is being conducted at the church, prepare the meeting room; if in a home, call the hostess to confirm and work out any further details. If this study is being conducted in a retreat setting, make certain that refreshments are available and that the space will be conducive to good learning.

• Provide paper, pencils and extra copies of *Taking the Next Step: A Guide for New Church Members.*

• Read through the member books, noting places where you will need to know current information about your church.

• On poster board or a large sheet of paper, print five functions of the church: *Evangelism,*

Discipleship, Ministry, Fellowship, Worship.

• Prepare a minilecture reviewing the functions of the church. For more information, see *Kingdom Principles for Church Growth,* by Gene Mims.

PROCEDURE:

1. As members arrive, allow time for participants to greet each other, visit together, and enjoy light refreshments.

2. Read the purpose statement for chapter 2, "What Is the Church?" Review briefly the material that was studied in the first session. Ask if there are any questions about that material.

3. Give a minilecture on the five functions of the church, referring to the poster as you speak. Allow time for the participants to fill in the blanks in each of the sections that deal with the functions of the church. (Make sure that the information given is accurate for your particular church.) Allow time for discussion of each one as you move along.

4. Refer to the qualities of believers as identified by Gene Getz (under the section, "The Church Will Help You Grow in Spiritual Maturity"). If time permits, expand on the ten qualities by sharing with members the following biblical information about each quality:
• *Having a good reputation*—With fellow believers: "He was well spoken of by the brethren who were at Lystra and Iconium" (Acts 16:2).
With unbelievers: "Moreover he must have a good testimony among those who are outside, lest he fall into reproach and the snare of the devil" (1 Tim. 3:7).

- *Being worthy of respect*—Paul instructed deacons and their wives to be reverent (1 Tim. 3:8, 11). He told Titus to be reverent (Titus 2:7-8a). He used a Greek term that meant they were to be dignified and handle themselves in such a way that they would command respect.

- *Being morally pure*—Paul was concerned that all Christian men and women maintain morally pure relationships. Personal moral purity is to be a hallmark of our faith. (See 1 Thess. 4:3-7.)

- *Guarding our words*—Paul warned us to guard against what we say that may be intended to hurt or harm (1 Tim. 3:11; Titus 2:3).

- *Guarding our tempers*—Paul warned about sinful anger. Anger is not classified as sin unless it is a result of uncontrolled temper (Jas. 1:19-20) or when it lingers and becomes a basis for revenge or harm. This kind of anger becomes an evil (Rom. 12:17).

- *Being temperate*—Paul described a quality of maturity as being in control. This control is based on faith in God that gives calm in the midst of anything that happens. (See 1 Tim. 3:2; Titus 2:2; 1 Thess. 5:8.)

- *Being sober minded*—Paul instructed Christians to be people of good judgment. Good judgment begins with a proper view of yourself. Sober-mindedness includes having a clear understanding of God's grace as the source of our salvation, our usefulness to God, and any good that may come from our lives. Another aspect of sober mindedness is *meekness*. To be meek is to be clearly under God's authority and presence. (See 1 Tim. 3:2; Titus 1:8; Titus 2:2; Titus 2:6.)

- *Being generous*—Paul reminded us that everything we have comes from God. Our possessions are opportunities for hospitality and help.

- *Free from addictions.*—Paul is speaking to

addiction to wine in 1 Timothy 3:3,8 and Titus 1:7; 2:3. The problem of addictive behavior is seen today in gambling, drugs, food, tobacco, and many other things.

• *Able to teach*—Paul's wisdom about teaching as a spiritual quality is best understood in 2 Timothy 2:23.

5. When discussing the "Ministry" section of the book, give to each person a copy of the budget, committee information, volunteer jobs, and any other information you have gathered to show them how your church participates in ministry and missions.

6. Distribute copies of your church's mission statement. Consider asking your pastor or another church leader to explain what the statement means to the life of your church, and how the church carries out its mission. If possible, explain the process of how/why the mission statement was written. If there is not one in existence, encourage members to write one on page 12, then ask volunteers to share what they wrote. (It is always appropriate to focus on the Great Commission.) Emphasize the importance of each member doing his or her part to carry out this vision of your church.

7. Ask members to turn to the glossary at the back of the book. Briefly review the terms that apply to this second session and ask if there are any questions or comments about each one. Clarify the definitions, if necessary.

8. Close this session by asking each person to tell something that your church has done in ministry to them or to share why they chose to join your church. (To encourage sharing, tell of some times in your church life when you have been ministered to by the church and its members.)

ANSWERS FOR CHAPTER 2:

Matthew 28:19-20—*(go)*, *(make disciples)*, *(baptizing)*, *(teaching);* 2 Timothy 2:23—*(Lord's servant)*, *(kind)*, *(teach)*, *(resentful);*
Page 16—Ministry through *support groups, recovery groups, seminars in parenting, financial management, etc*; Acts 2:46-47—*(meet together)*, *(glad)*, *(sincere)*, *(praising God);* Acts 2:42—*(teaching)*, *(fellowship)*, *(bread)*, *(prayer)*;
1 Corinthians 1:10—*(perfectly united)*;
Genesis 28:16-17—*(Lord)*, *(house of God)*.

HOW DOES A CHURCH WORK?

PREPARATION:

• If this class is being conducted at the church, prepare the meeting room; if in a home, call the hostess to confirm and work out any further details. If this study is being conducted in a retreat setting, make certain that refreshments are available and that the space will be conducive to good learning.

• Provide paper, pencils and extra copies of *Taking the Next Step: A Guide for New Church Members.*

• Consult with your church staff to compile a list of all the things your church does to provide opportunities for the spiritual development of its members. (*Examples: Sunday School, weekday Bible study groups, cell groups, Vacation Bible School, Winter Bible study, congregational studies on Wednesday or Sunday evenings, Discipleship Training, discipleship groups, retreats for Bible study and spiritual growth, and so forth.*)

• Obtain enough copies of *The Baptist Faith and Message* for each participant to receive one. (These are available at your Baptist Book Store, item #9201-72.)

• Prepare a statement or list of the qualifications for membership in your church.

- Research the ordinances of your church (baptism and the Lord's Supper). Find out how often they are held, who is responsible for the planning, who is responsible for leading in the services, and so on.

- Make a list of your church's key leaders. Include members of the staff, deacons, major committee chairmen, and volunteer leadership. Identify their functions in the church and the qualifications for holding those positions.

PROCEDURE:

1. As members arrive, allow time for participants to visit together and have snacks, if provided.

2. Read the purpose statement for chapter 3, "How Does the Church Work?" Review briefly the material that was studied in the previous session. Ask if there are any questions about that material.

3. Distribute copies of *The Baptist Faith and Message*. This will be a particularly helpful resource for new Christians or those new to the Baptist faith. State that the basic resource for your church is the Bible. Read aloud the statement from *The Baptist Faith and Message* that is printed on page 21. Ask for volunteers to share titles of some of the member/student books they use in Bible study. Point out that the curriculum is biblically based, educationally sound, and person-centered.

4. Discuss how your church is organized to help its members' spiritual growth and development. (*In addition to Sunday morning Bible study, the staff— pastor, minister of education, minister of youth—*

schedules Discipleship Training classes, retreats, and other training events.) Direct members to use the margin on page 22 to list specific events (*Winter Bible Study, Vacation Bible School, Associational Training Sessions, and so on*) that your church provides. Compare with the list you made to be sure nothing is omitted. Allow time for sharing and discussing.

5. Give to each person a copy of the membership requirements of your church. Explain the importance of each of these requirements and how your church developed them.

6. Give a minilecture on the ordinances of baptism and the Lord's Supper. Explain the way your church observes these ordinances so that members can fill in the blanks in each of the sections relating to the ordinances. Ask if anyone has a question about baptism or the Lord's Supper and their participation in these observances. Answer all questions as best you can—if there are questions you can't answer, promise the group that you will find out the answers before your next meeting.

7. Call on volunteers to read the Scripture passages listed in the member books under the section "The Lord's Supper." (*Matt. 26:26-28; Luke 22:19; 1 Cor. 11:25; 10:16-17.*)

8. Give each person a copy of the list of key church leaders. Ask members to turn to the section "The Leadership of the Church" and complete the exercises there. Be available to answer questions or provide additional information they may need. Allow time for them to complete the assignment.

9. Discuss the requirements for volunteer leaders and their importance to the functions of the church. Explain your church's process of enlisting workers (*through the nominating committee, division directors, or whatever*) and its expectations for volunteer leaders. Explain that in the next session they will be given information about spiritual gifts; and each person will begin to determine what his or her spiritual gift is, so that they may better serve the church.

10. Close this session by asking members to list some areas of your church where they feel they might be interested in working. Pray that God will help each member to ascertain his or her place of service, and that they will feel His call to serve.

ANSWERS FOR CHAPTER 3:

John 6: 28-29—*(believe)*; John 1:29—*(Lamb of God)*; Page 25—The Lord's Supper Scriptures—*past; death; Savior; sin; hope; future; salvation; death; sin; resurrection;*
1 Corinthians 10:16-17—*(unity)*;
John 10:34—*(sheep), (voice), (his own), (voice.);*
1 Timothy 3:8-13—(*worthy of respect, sincere*) *(wine), (gain), (against them), (temperate)* and *(trustworthy); (children), (household);* Ephesians 4:11-12— *(apostles), (prophets), (evangelists), (pastors* and *teachers).*

WHAT CAN I DO?

PREPARATION:

• If this class is being conducted at the church, prepare the meeting room; if in a home, call the hostess to confirm and work out any further details. If this study is being conducted in a retreat setting, make certain that refreshments are available and that the space will be conducive to good learning.

• Provide paper, pencils and extra copies of *Taking the Next Step: A Guide for New Church Members.*

• During this session, participants will be introduced to the concept of spiritual gifts. The member book contains a spiritual gifts inventory, "What Do I Have to Offer?" reprinted from *Countdown: 20 Bible Studies for High School Seniors.* Carefully read through the list and directions for scoring so you will be familiar with the material. (This is not meant to be an exhaustive study; for more information, a good resource is *Serving God: Discovering and Using Your Spiritual Gifts,* by Ken Hemphill, Sampson Ministry Resources, Distributed by the Sunday School Board.)

• Check with your pastor or minister of education to see if job descriptions are available. If so, obtain or make copies to be distributed in class. If not available, compile a list of the jobs that are filled by volunteers at your church.
• Enlist two persons who have been faithful in their volunteer ministry at your church; ask them to

be prepared to give a three-minute testimony on the importance of finding a place to become connected to the church. (You might consider including a newer member of the congregation so that class members will see that it is good for newcomers to get involved quickly).

• Allow plenty of time for participants to complete the spiritual gifts inventory ("What Do I Have to Offer?") and to chart the results.

PROCEDURE:

1. As members arrive, allow time for participants to greet each other and have some refreshments, if provided.

2. Read the purpose statement for chapter 4, "What Can I Do?" Review briefly the content and major emphases of the previous three sessions. Allow time for questions from the preceding material; answer as many questions as possible.

3. Call for a volunteer to read 1 Corinthians 12:12-20. Begin session 4 by pointing out the significance of understanding that the church is the body of Christ, and that each of the participants is a major part in this body; emphasize the uniqueness of each person. Allow time for members to fill in the information called for in the first section of chapter 4 of *Taking the Next Step: A Guide for New Church Members*.

4. Distribute paper and pencils, then ask each person to list some ways they believe God wants to use them in your church.
Allow time for them to complete their lists, then discuss the role that obedience plays in the life of a

Christian. Introduce the two volunteer workers who are going to speak to the group. Allow each speaker to share what service in the church has meant to them through the years, and how it has helped their spiritual growth and development.

4. Call for a volunteer to read aloud 1 Peter 4:10-11 and another to read aloud 1 Corinthians 12:4. After they have finished, read aloud the definition of spiritual gifts (page 31)—*the skills and abilities that God gives through His Spirit to all Christians that equip Christians to serve God in the Christian community.* Explain that for the remainder of this session you will be studying about spiritual gifts.
  Be sure each member has a pencil and a copy of *Taking the Next Step: A Guide for New Church Members.* Ask participants to turn to the spiritual gifts inventory ("What Do I Have to Offer?") in chapter 4. Read the instructions aloud, then allow them to begin work on the inventory. As they work, be available to answer questions or clarify the process, if necessary.

  Explanations of the twelve spiritual gifts used for this inventory:
  1. Prophecy—Strong verbal abilities; feels God's leadership in speaking; direct and to the point in conversation; controversial and often misunderstood; aims at the heart of problems; interested in politics, public concerns, and world issues.
  2. Service—Closely tuned to everyday needs of persons; desires to be helpful in specific, concrete ways; warm, caring, and loving; levelheaded in crisis situations; low visibility; works in the background as a support and strength to more prominent leaders.
  3. Teaching—Desire to speak truth in ways that nur-

ture growth; capacity to analyze, explain, and interpret facts; levelheaded; ability to focus on problems and issues; willingness to "be an example" for others.

4. *Exhorting*—Capacity for stirring and inspiring speech; sensitive to others' problems and dilemmas; provides revealing answers that others find helpful; confrontational, but not offensive; long-suffering and patient with the weakness of others.

5. *Sharing*—Appreciation for simple and natural things; willing to share material possessions, open in sharing personal experience-particularly in relation to one's faith, in touch with inner feelings and an ability to communicate these feelings to others; satisfaction from sharing one's resources freely.

6. *Leading*—Interested in organization and delegation; ability to see needs and provide leadership in meeting needs; hardworking; giving attention to detail; concerned about directions that are according to the "purposes and will of God."

7. *Mercy*—Compassionate and caring; bearing others' burdens; sensing in others the emotions of pain, affliction, and despair; action-oriented; a readiness of mind to help those who are weak; a feeling of happiness that comes from doing merciful deeds.

8. *Love*—Capacity for intimacy and closeness; feelings of affection toward many people; a desire to be in harmony with others; ability to give without expectation of return; orientation to practical needs of others; a belief that people are "one big family."

9. *Enthusiasm*—Highly motivated; ability to bring "sparkle" and excitement to a situation; unusual capacity to be caught up and absorbed in a task; intense and emotional; feeling of adventure about past, present, and future events.

10. *Hope*—Sensitive and aware of spiritual concerns;

optimistic about other persons' motives and actions; not easily disappointed in persons; ability to bounce back; strong in difficult situations; patient in time of trouble.

11. Prayer—Capacity to express affection and love in simple ways; childlike, playful, and spontaneous, lacking in self-consciousness; ability to put into words what that "heart" is saying.

12. Hospitality—Outgoing, informal, and friendly; a "welcoming" attitude to friends and strangers alike; ability to help others feel "at home" in all kinds of situations; desire to do things for others with no thought of return.

After they have completed the inventory, guide the participants to score the results in the 12 charts provided in their member book, to total the scores, and complete the triangle graph as directed. Then share the descriptions of the 12 gifts as written above.

5. Wrap up the inventory by pointing out that the purpose of learning about our spiritual gifts is to use them in service to God. These gifts should be used wisely and prayerfully.

6. Close this session with a time of silent prayer. Call for each participant to ask God to reveal His will for them as part of the body of Christ. Then pray aloud that each person will be willing to accept a place of service as God leads them.

ANSWERS FOR CHAPTER 4:

1 Corinthians 12:12-20—(*unit*), (*parts*), (*one body*), (*Spirit*), (*body*); Romans 12:4-5—(*one*), (*many*), (*function*), (*many*), (*one*), (*member*), (*all*); 1 Peter 4:10-11—(*others*), (*speaks*), (*serves*); 1 Corinthians 12:4—(*Spirit*), (*Lord*), (*God*); 1 Corinthians 12:31-13:1—(*most excellent*), (*men*), (*angels*), (*love*).

WHERE DO I START?

PREPARATION:

• Since this is the last session of the study, plan to serve simple refreshments and spend some time visiting together.

• On poster board or a large piece of paper, write an outline of *Taking the Next Step: A Guide for New Church Members* by listing the titles of the five chapters: (*Who Am I? What Is the Church? How Does the Church Work? What Can I Do? Where Do I Start?*) Post the outline on a focal wall.

• On poster board or a large piece of paper, write the five questions found under the section entitled "Make Your Commitment." (*What convictions from God fill my heart? What abilities has God given me? What are my real interests? What are some church needs I see? What would Jesus do?*)

• Prepare a summary minilecture that will recap the main points of the first four sessions of this study.

• Provide paper and pencils for everyone.

PROCEDURE:

1. Refer to the poster on the wall that outlines *Taking the Next Step: A Guide for New Church Members*. Read the purpose statement for chapter 5, "Where Do I Start?" Briefly review the previous four

sessions, showing how they fit together for this last session.

2. Give a minilecture on the fact that Christians are happiest and most able to serve God with enthusiasm when they ensure they are plugged in to three essential connections: *A connection with God; a connection with others; and a connection with God's purpose.* Explain that in this session you will be reviewing some of the roles to be filled in your church. Ask that they begin to think about how these essential connections speak to them personally.

3. Read aloud the story of the turtle on the fencepost from chapter 5 of the book. State that God will provide our needs for service through Him. Ask a volunteer to complete the Scripture from Philippians 4:13.

4. Point out the importance of the support provided by other Christians and fellow church members. Emphasize the fact that we need relationships that are vertical (*with God*) and horizontal (*with other persons*), and call attention to the fact that church dropouts often occur when a person is not part of a circle of friends at church.
Direct members to list on a sheet of paper the names of some persons in the congregation to whom they feel a special connection. Ask them to identify the connection and how it can help them to find God's place of service for them. Allow time for discussion.

5. Share with the group how people are enlisted to work in your church. Explain the roles of the nominating committee, church council, and Sunday

School council. Briefly review the opportunities for service that are listed under "Your Opportunities to Serve Christ Through His Church" in chapter 5. (*Some examples are: Age group classes in Sunday School or Discipleship Training; Ministry opportunities such as music, outreach, telephone, or prayer chains.*) Ask for any additions to these lists and instruct members to write these in the margins of the book.

6. Ask participants to refer to the "Make Your Commitment" poster on the wall and to write down their responses to the five questions. After most have finished, remind them that little things are important, and guide them as they fill in the response space in the book, "The Service of Little Noticed Things."

7. Remind the participants that each person is needed and wanted in the work of your church. Share the research information in the book that says you will feel satisfied with your church if: You become involved in the ministries of your church; you become a part of a group of three or more people that you can consider friends; you become a disciple who leads others to accept Christ and helps them develop into maturing Christians.

8. As a closing exercise, ask members to read the statement in the book under "A Confession and a Commitment" and to prayerfully sign their name in the blank.

9. Dismiss with a prayer of thanksgiving for these new church members and their commitment to serve God in your church.

ANSWERS FOR CHAPTER 5:

Philippians 4:13—(_everything_), (_him_);
1 John 3:7-8—(_right_), (_sinful_), (_destroy_), (_devil_);
2 Peter 1:5-7—(_goodness_), (_knowledge_), (_self-control_), (_perseverance_), (_godliness_), (_brotherly kindness_), (_love_).

CHRISTIAN GROWTH STUDY PLAN
PREPARING CHRISTIANS TO GROW

In the **Christian Growth Study Plan (formerly Church Study Course),** the member's book, *Taking the Next Step, A Guide for New Church Members* is a resource for course credit in the subject area "The Church" of the Christian Growth category of diploma plans. To receive credit, read the book, complete the learning activities, show your work to your pastor, a staff member or church leader, then complete the following information.

Send this completed page to the Christian Growth Study Plan, 127 Ninth Avenue, North, MSN 117, Nashville, TN 37234-0117. This page may be duplicated. FAX: (615)251-5067 (When duplicating for a group or individual study, please use pages 31-32 of this book instead of what is found in *Taking the Next Step.***)**

For information about the Christian Growth Study Plan, refer to the current Christian Growth Study Plan Catalog. Your church office may have a copy. If not, request a free copy from the Christian Growth Study Plan office (615/251-2525).

TAKING THE NEXT STEP Course Number: CG-0376

PARTICIPANT INFORMATION

Social Security Number ‑ ‑

Personal CGSP Number*

Name (First, MI, Last)

☐ Mr.   ☐ Miss
☐ Mrs.

Address (Street, Route, or P.O. Box)

Home Phone ‑

Date of Birth ‑ ‑

City, State

Zip Code

CHURCH INFORMATION

Church Name

Address (Street, Route, or P. O. Box)

City, State

Zip Code

CHANGE REQUEST ONLY

☐ Former Name

City, State

Zip Code

☐ Former Address

City, State

Zip Code

☐ Former Church

Signature of Pastor, Conference Leader, or Other Church Leader

Date

*New participants are requested but not required to give SS# and date of birth. Existing participants, please give CGSP# when using SS# for the first time. Thereafter, only one ID# is required.

Mail to: Christian Growth Study Plan, 127 Ninth Avenue, North, MSN 117, Nashville, TN 37234-0117. FAX: (615) 251-5067